W9-CFI-992

·SUPERBOOK·

GAMES
TO MAKE AND PLAY

PIA HSIAO, NEIL LORIMER
& NICK WILLIAMS

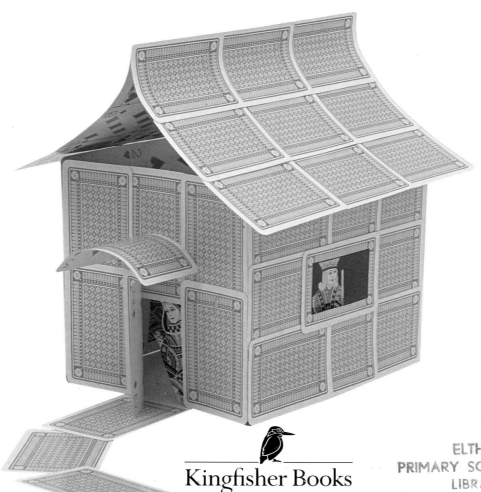

Kingfisher Books

Contents

A word of warning: to make some of the games in this book requires the use of a saw or cutting tool, and hammer and nails. **Always** ask an adult to help you with any difficult cutting or hammering, and **always** take great care.

Kingfisher Books, Grisewood & Dempsey Ltd,
Elsley House, 24–30 Great Titchfield Street,
London W1P 7AD

This revised edition published in 1987 by Kingfisher Books
Originally published in hard cover in 1975
10 9 8 7 6 5 4

BRITISH LIBRARY CATALOGUING IN PUBLICATION DATA
Hsiao, Pia
    The superbook of games to make and play. —
    Rev. ed. — (Kingpins).
    1. Indoor games — Design and construction
    —Juvenile literature
    I. Title II. Lorimer, Neil III. Williams,
    Nick IV. Games you make and play
    745.592   GV1230

ISBN 0-86272-315-9

Phototypeset by Southern Positives and Negatives (SPAN), Lingfield, Surrey
Printed in Hong Kong by South China Printing Company

Games

This book will not only show you how to play a variety of both familiar and unusual games, it will also help you to design and construct them for yourself. Anyone with a simple knowledge of woodwork can experience the satisfaction of making their own Darts board or Backgammon set; other games require only paper, glue and scissors.

The things you need to play many games – a board, counters and dice – can be made in different ways, the suggestions here are only the beginning and you can think up other ideas for yourself. Rules, with simple diagrams, are at the end of the book. You may find some surprises – did you know for instance that there are many different versions of the game Draughts?

Many of the games in this book are very old and have changed little through the centuries. Some like Roll a Penny were, and are still, fairground games, others such as Darts and Shove Ha'penny originated as pub games. Draughts or Checkers has a complicated history dating from AD 1100. It combines elements from Chess, Backgammon, and a Moorish game Alquerque. But whatever the game all you need to play is a little skill and some luck. Have fun!

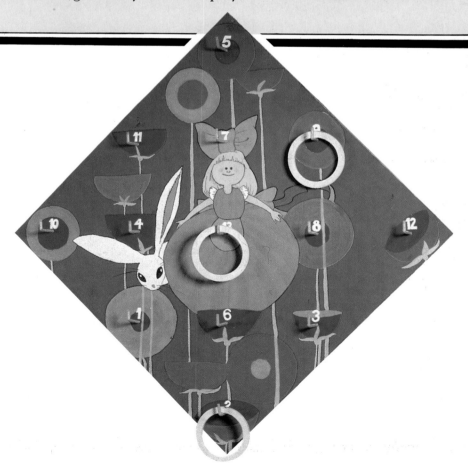

Making Games Boards

You will need
plywood or pine board
2 hinges
saw
screwdriver
glue
sandpaper
panel pins
hammer

1 Simple Hinged Box

The dimensions of your box will depend upon the number and size of pieces you want to store in it. Cut 6 pieces of pine as shown.

Fix the 4 sides and the bottom together with glue and panel pins.

Fit the lid with hinges which should be recessed into the sides and lid as shown.

Sandpaper the box and paint or varnish it. You may like to decorate it.

2 Box with Drop-in Lid

Again choose a shape and size to suit the pieces you want to store in it. Cut out the 4 sides from pine.
Fix them together with panel pins and glue.

Cut 2 pieces of plywood to fit *inside* the box. Nail and glue one piece in as the bottom.

Cut another piece of plywood the same size as the *outside* of the box.

Glue the other inside fitting piece underneath it so it drops into the box as a lid.

Trim the box lid. Sandpaper and paint or varnish the box.

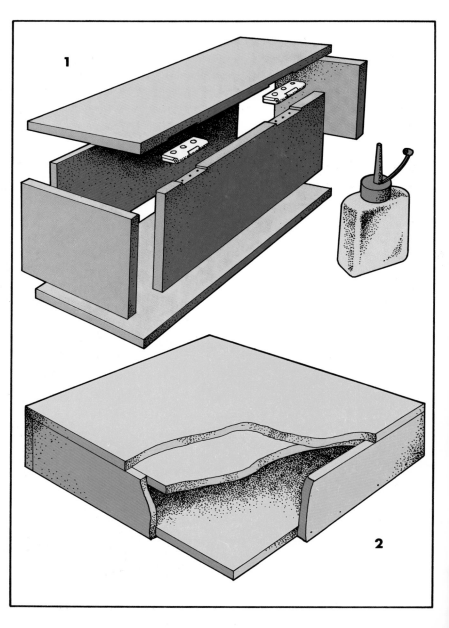

You will need:
2 pieces of heavy card
(about 36 × 18 cm)
strong sticky tape
sheet of decorative paper
sheet of plain paper or
light card
cutting tool
glue

A Games Board

1 Cut the 2 pieces of card to about the dimensions shown. This is the average size of many board games.

2 Lay the pieces together and tape over the join to form a hinge. This is the inside of the board.

3 Fold the board over and tape along the back of it.

4 Cut the ends of the tape as shown and fold it over inside.

5 Strengthen and protect the edges of the board with tape.

6 Glue a piece of decorative paper or plastic adhesive material to each outside surface.

7 Glue the board surface for the actual game on to the inside in one piece.
You make this on paper or light card and if necessary you can score it lightly to ensure a good fit.

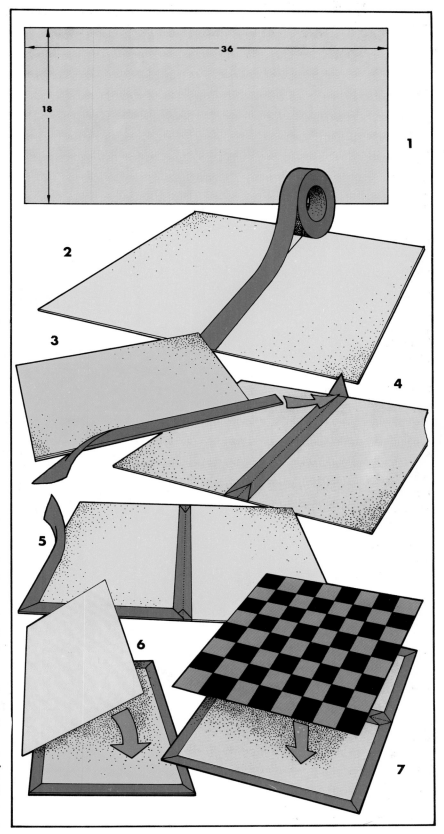

Markers

You will need
stiff card
adhesive stars
lengths of rod
pebbles
bottle tops
nuts and bolts
cork bottle tops
toothpicks
paper
self-setting clay (Das)
plastic toy figures
shells
poster paint
enamel paint
paint brushes

1 Card shapes
Cut out several sizes of each shape in card. Glue them on top of each other. Paint each counter in a different colour of poster paint.

2 Clay pieces
Roll out a piece of self-setting clay. Cut shapes from it and paint them.

3 Rod counters
Cut a slanting piece from a length of rod (such as a broom handle). Paint the uprights all the same colour with poster paint. Paint the slanting faces in contrasting colours with enamel paint.

4 Pebbles
Clean the pebbles thoroughly. Enamel them all over in one colour. Decorate them in a contrasting colour.

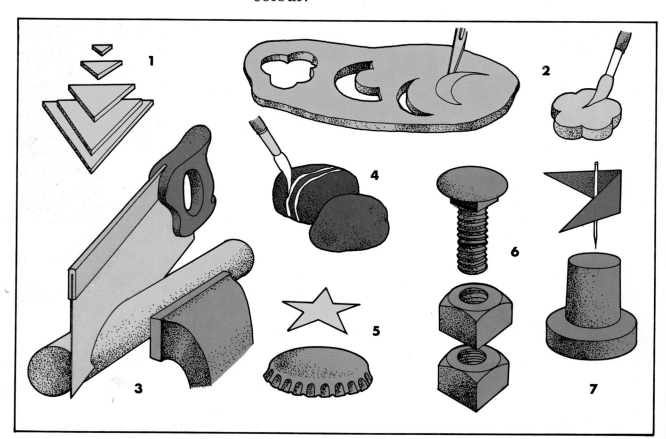

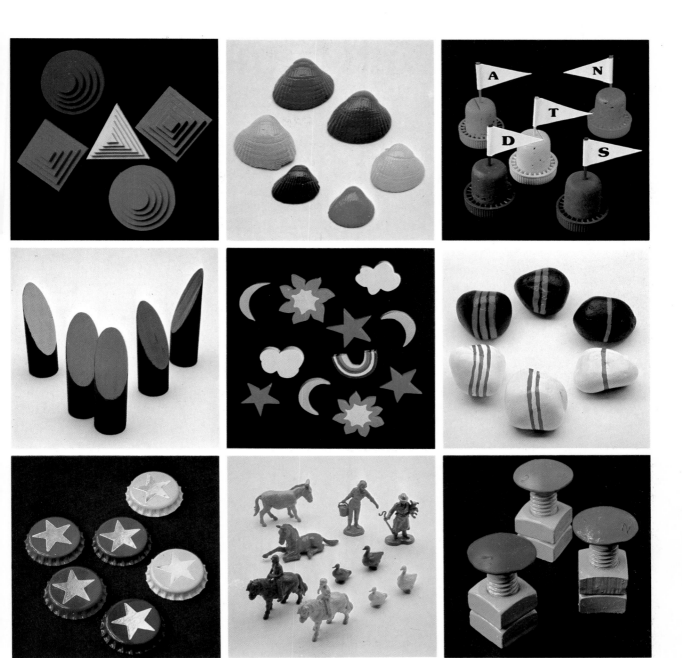

5 Bottle top counters
Enamel the bottle tops. Fix a silver star or other shape to each.

6 Nuts and bolts
Screw two nuts to each bolt, so they will stand firmly. Paint them in enamel with contrasting colours.

7 Waving the flag
Paint cork bottle tops in poster paints.

Glue paper flags onto toothpicks and fix one into the top of each cork. Write the initial or number of each player on the flags.

8 People and animals
Paint the plastic farm figures all over with enamel paints.

9 Shell counters
Paint shells in different colours.

7

Dice and Spinners

You will need
self-setting clay (Das)
4 × 4 × 4 cm wood
light card
5 mm dowel
large wooden bead
18 drawing pins
adhesive numbers
   and letters
heavy card
15 × 20 cm chipboard
13 cm length of wood
2 beads
nail
saw
drill
glue
pencil sharpener

1 **Clay dice** Mould and sandpaper clay into cube. Paint cube. Paint on numbers.
2 **Wooden dice** Cut and sandpaper 4 cm wooden cube. Drill holes 1–6. Paint.
3 **Card teetotum** Cut out and paint card. Fix on numbers. Fold and glue. Sharpen 5 cm length of dowel, paint and push through centre of spinner.
4 **Dice ball** Fix drawing pins into the wooden bead. Fix three groups of adhesive numbers 1–6 on the drawing pin heads.
5 **Spinner** Cut spinner star from card. Paint and fix on numbers. Sharpen 9 cm length of dowel, paint and push through spinner.
6 **Rainbow spinner** Cut and decorate chipboard base. Sharpen and paint pointer. Fix pointer between 2 wooden beads in centre of circle so that it spins freely

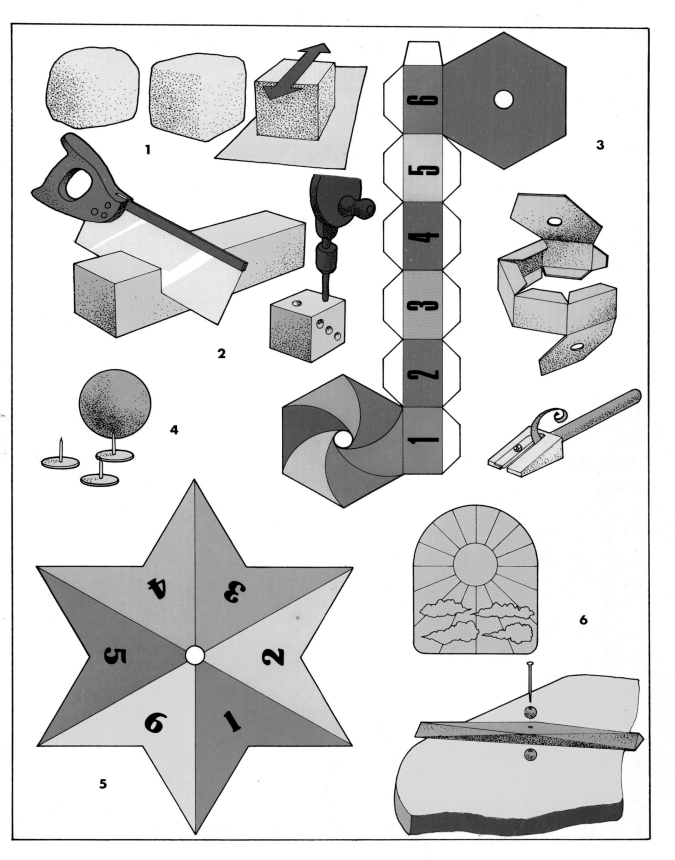

9

Solitaire

You will need
heavy card
piece of cloth
soup plate
2 large elastic bands
32 acorns, hazel nuts or
    marbles
compass
pencil
cutting tool
scissors
glue
paint
paint brush

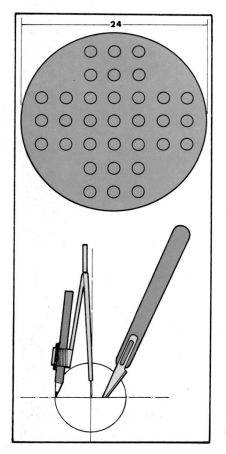

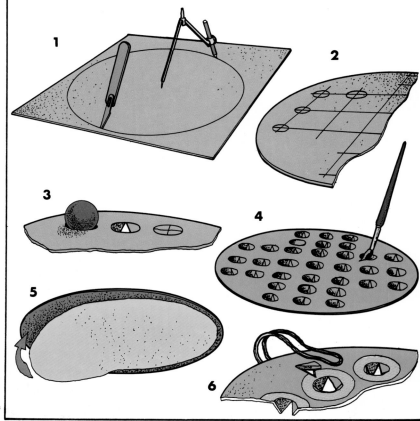

The board

1 Using the compass, draw a circle the size of the soup plate on the card. Cut it out.
2 Mark out the holes using the compass as shown on the diagram.
3 Cut out the holes so that the marbles will sit on them.
4 Paint the board, painting decorative circles round the holes.
5 Cut a circle of cloth and glue it to the back of the board.

6 Cut 4 V-shaped nicks on the board. Pass the rubber bands under the bowl from one side to the other to hold the board in position on the bowl. Store the marbles in the bowl.

The pieces

7 If you are using nuts or acorns paint them with enamel paint or varnish to preserve them.

The rules are on *page 35.*

Snakes and Ladders

You will need
heavy card
light card
60 circular stickers
pencil
cutting tool
paint
paint brush
glue

1 Draw the board on the heavy card to the dimensions shown. Cut it out.

2 Paint the board. Outline the track.

3 Paint and number the stickers. Fix them in place on the board.

4 and 5 Cut out the snakes and ladders in varying lengths and stick them on the board.

Players move round the board towards Home according to the throw of the dice. If a piece lands on a ladder it climbs it; on a snake, it slides down it.

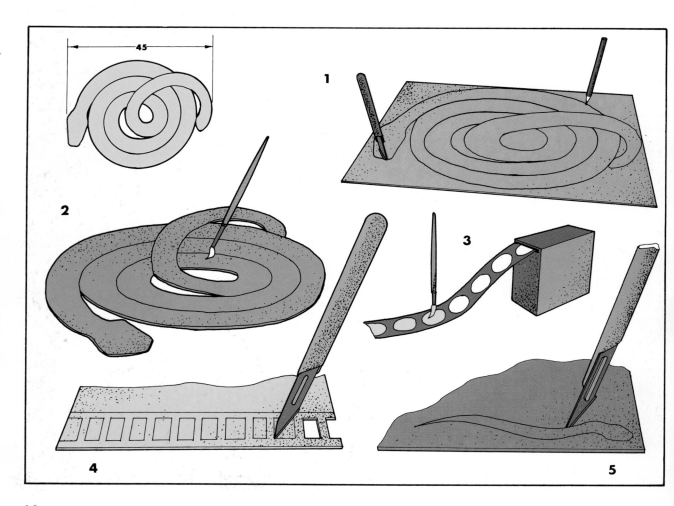

Queen's Guard

You will need
card
adhesive stickers
2 bolts
14 nuts
cutting tool
coloured pencils
paint
paint brush

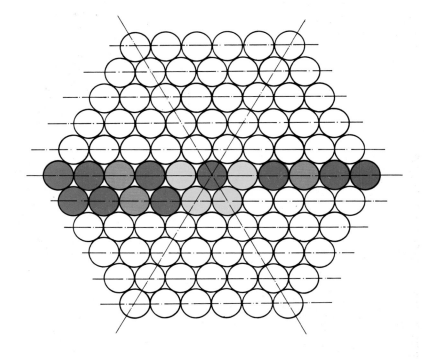

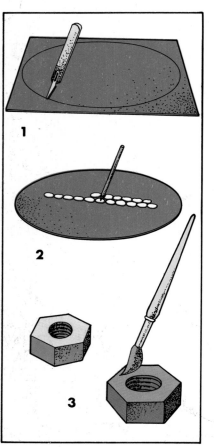

The board
1 Cut out a circle of card with a radius of about 20 cm.
2 To form the hexagonal playing area, first stick down 11 stickers in a straight line across the centre of the circle of card as shown in the diagram above. On the adjoining line stick down 10 stickers. Continue to work in lines like this until the design of half the board is complete.

Stick on stickers in the same way to make the other half of the board match and form the complete hexagon.

Colour the stickers in circles from the centre with the coloured pencils, as shown in the picture.

The men
3 Paint 7 nuts and 1 bolt in one colour and the rest in another colour with enamel paint.

Screw one nut of each set onto a bolt to make the Queen.

The other nuts of each set are the Queen's Guard.

The rules for the game of Queen's Guard are given on *page 35.*

The original board for Queen's Guard is a hexagon made up of hexagonal sections, like a honeycomb. This game appears to be based on the structure of a beehive with the worker bees protecting their Queen.

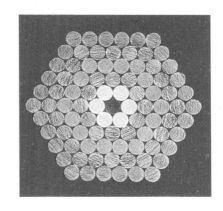

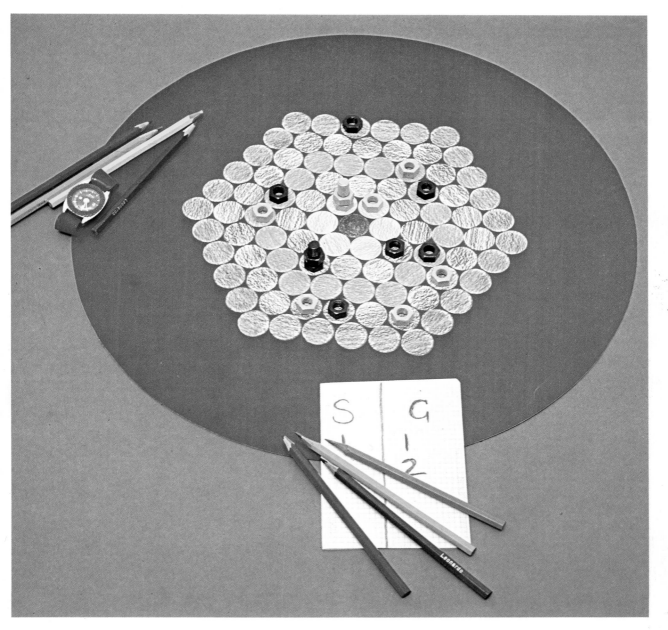

Draughts

You will need

8 pieces of wood
45 × 5 × 375 mm
36 × 36 cm canvas or strong cloth
large dowel or broom handle
large cardboard tube (about 11 cm diameter)
small tube (about 4 cm diameter)
card
paint and paint brush
vice or sawing board
saw
glue
transparent tape

The board

1 Divide each piece of wood into 8 squares. Paint them alternate colours.
2 Glue the strips to the canvas with PVA glue.

The draughtsmen and containers

3 Cut 24 counters from the dowel. Paint them.
4 The large tube is for storage; the small one for the counters. For the lids and bases, cut card circles. Draw circles the size of the tubes in the centres. Cut to these circles. Fold and tape the sides. Tape on the bases. Paint the containers.

The rules for Draughts are on *page 36*.

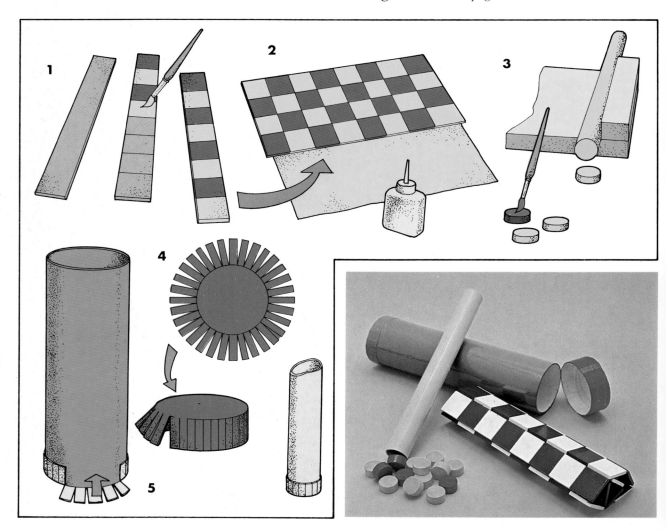

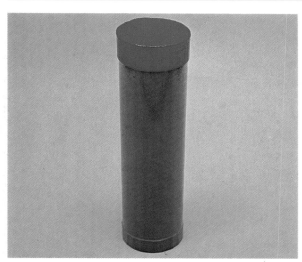

Backgammon

You will need

thin plywood
adhesive covering material
lengths of 1 cm × 1 cm wood
glue
nails
2 hinges
saw

cutting tool
felt in 2 colours
stiff paper in 2 colours
pen
ink
paint
paint brush

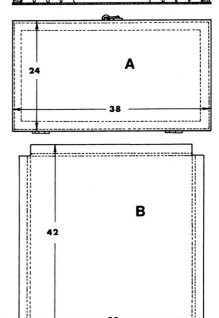

A

24

38

B

42

28

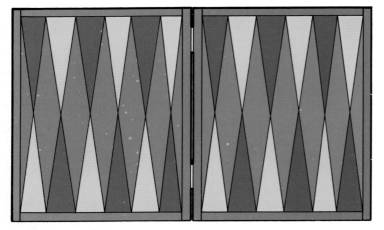

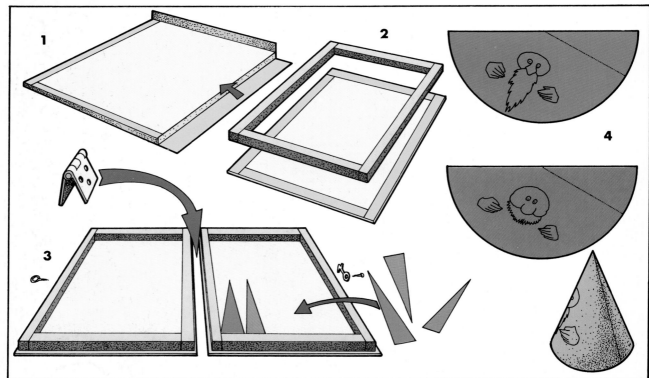

1

2

3

4

1 Cut out two pieces the size of A in plywood. Cover them in pieces the size of B in an adhesive material (such as Fablon).

2 Make 2 frames from lengths of 1 cm × 1 cm wood as shown ($37\frac{1}{2}$ cm for length, $21\frac{1}{2}$ cm for width). Fix with glue and small nails to the sides of the boards.

3 Fix small hinges to the sides of the boards to hold them together so that they will close like a flat box.

Lock the box with a hook and eye. Decorate the outside and edges of the box as shown on the diagram at the top of the page.
Cut 12 triangles of felt in one colour, 12 in the other. Use adhesive felt or glue the pieces in position as shown on the diagram and picture.

4 For the counters, make 15 semi-circles in each of the two colours of stiff paper. Glue them together to form small cones. Decorate them with pen and ink or paint.

The rules are given on *page 37.*

Mancala

You will need
2 bun tins
48 wooden beads
paint
paint brush
stiff card
decorative paper
ruler
pencil
cutting tool

The storage box
1 Cut the shape shown in pink from the card. Make cuts as shown and score along the dotted lines.
2 Fold the side flaps up.
3 Fold in the end and glue in position.
4 Complete the box so the board can slide into it. To cover the box, cut out the pink shape 1 cm larger all round and stick it over the completed box.

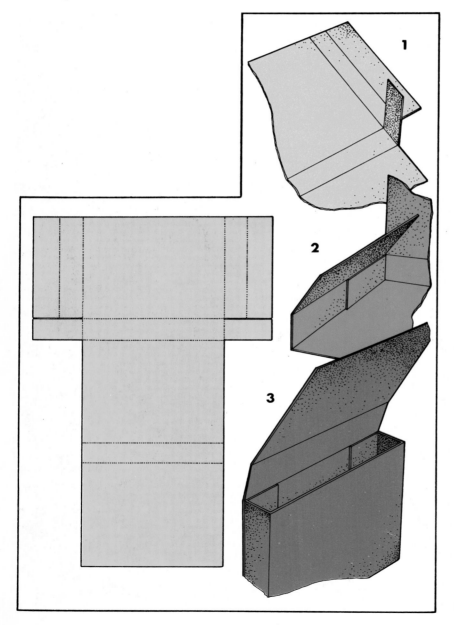

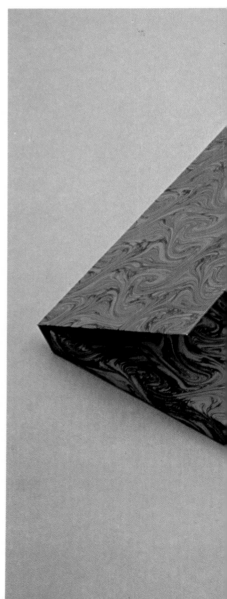

To make the board

Paint the bun tins as shown in the picture. You could add further decoration to the flat surfaces. Paint the beads if you wish.

The beads can be stored between the bun tins. The rules of Mancala are given on *page 38.*

This Nigerian Mancala board is carved in wood, with the design burnt into it. The game is played with seeds.

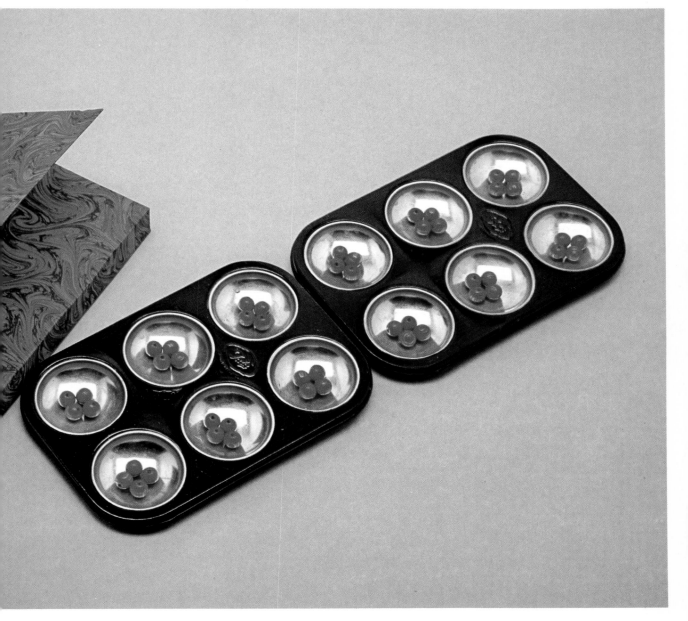

Word Fish

You will need
medium card
gift wrapping paper
old magazines
light card or paper
cutting tool
ruler
glue

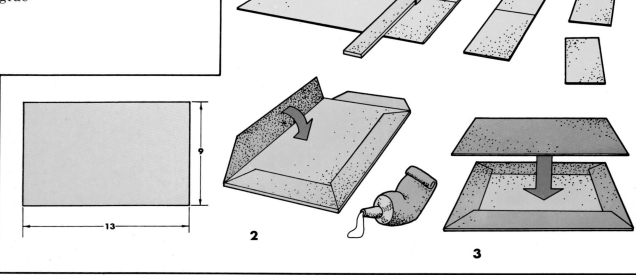

1 Cut cards the size of normal playing cards or larger, like the ones shown here.

2 Glue them to the back of wrapping paper. Cut out leaving 1 cm all round. Cut the corners and fold over.

3 Depending on how you want to use the cards (look at the rules on *page 38/39*), stick pictures or paper to the front of the cards. Use the plain cards for words, numbers or symbols.

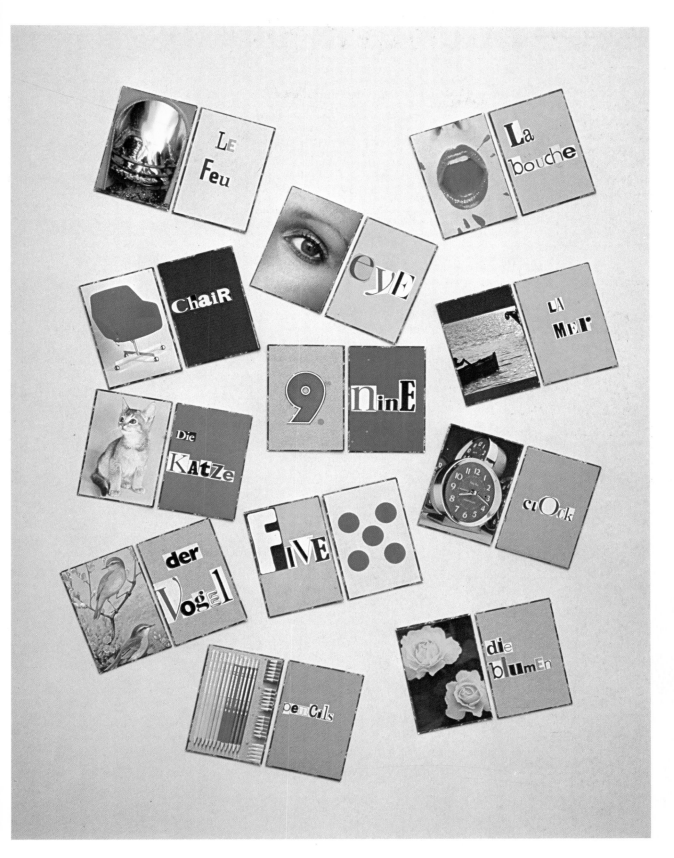

Shove Ha'penny

You will need
65 × 40 cm piece of 10 mm
    chipboard
2 pieces 40 × 50 cm of 20 mm
    softwood
54 flat-headed galvanised
    nails
white undercoat paint
paints
paint brush
masking tape
pencil
ruler
hacksaw
vice
wet and dry sandpaper
linseed oil
furniture wax

1 Paint all the wood in the undercoat.
Rule 9 stripes on the board 3 cm apart. Using masking tape, paint 4 stripes and the end areas. Paint a second coat and let it dry.
Remove tape, relay and paint remaining stripes. Using tape again, paint a 2 cm strip down each side. When dry, rub the surface with linseed oil and sandpaper. Wax and polish.

2 Drill holes in groups of 3 along both side strips and in one piece of softwood. Paint the 2 pieces of softwood to match the side strip. Glue to the board.

3 Cut the points off the nails. Paint half one colour and half another.

The rules are on *page 39.*

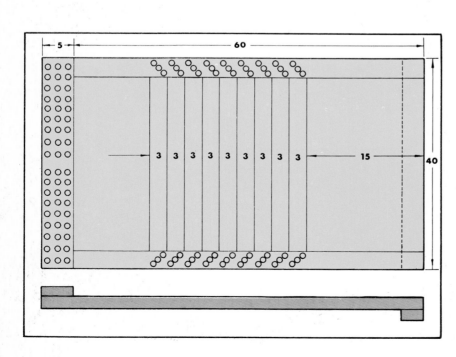

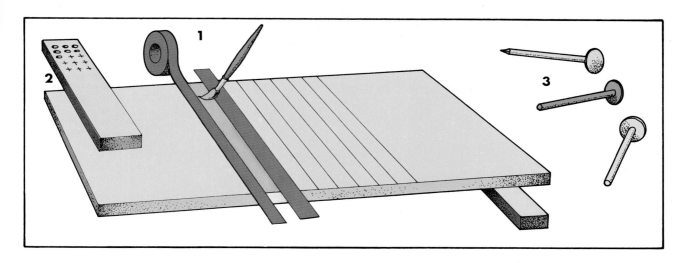

Roll a Penny

You will need
stiff card
coloured tape
pencil
ruler
number stencils
cutting tool
paint
paint brush
glue

The board
1 Cut 2 pieces of card as shown in yellow and blue. Score dotted lines. Rule the squares. Stencil in the numbers.
2 Fold and glue sides and end of yellow card.
3 Tape yellow and blue pieces together.

The shooters
4 For each shooter, cut 2 larger and 2 smaller pieces of card. Score and fold base card. Glue 2 small pieces for runner and fix between the side pieces.
5 When you are not using the board, it can be covered with the blue shooting area.

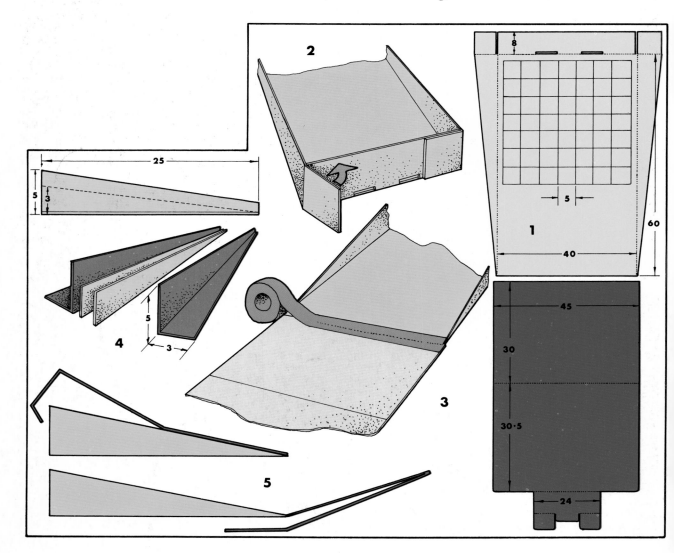

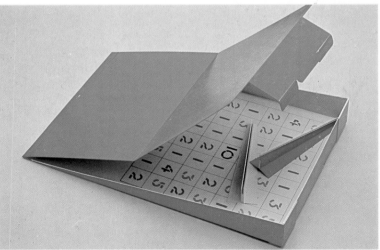

Flap Dice

You will need

pieces of pine or softwood
in following sizes:
9 pieces 30 × 50 × 20 mm (A)
3 pieces 320 × 50 × 20 mm (B)
2 pieces 360 × 50 × 20 mm (C)
36 × 36 cm hardboard
55 cm of 5 mm dowel
27 × 33 cm adhesive felt
45 round-headed mapping
   pins or adhesive
    numbers 1–9
drill
glue
nails

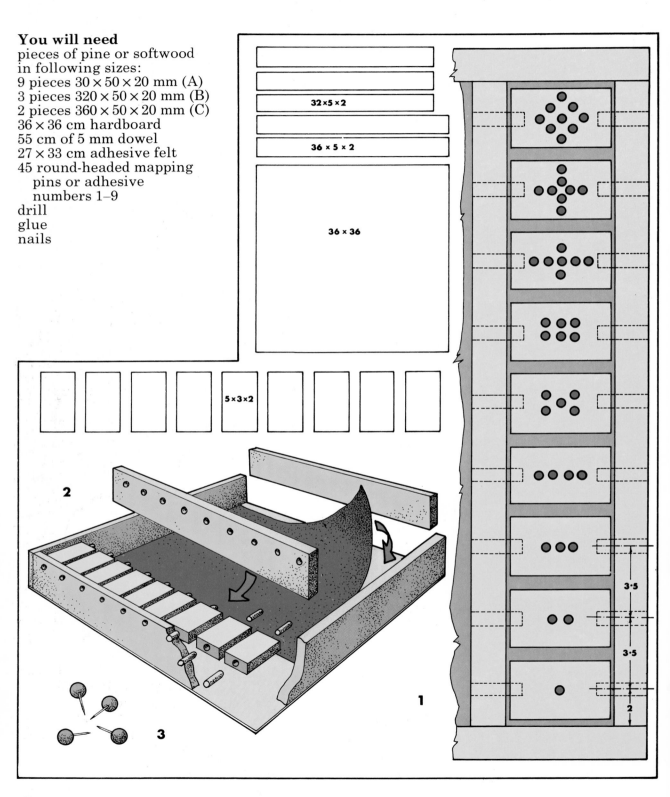

1 Drill 5 mm holes in the centre of the 3 cm blocks (A) approximately 10 mm deep. Take 2 pieces B and drill 7 mm holes 10 mm from top at distances shown in the diagram.
Cut 18 pieces of dowel 3 cm long. Glue into either end of the A pieces.

2 Nail the two pieces of wood C onto opposite sides of the hardboard. Now nail 2 B pieces (one with, one without holes) onto the other sides to form a box. Slide the 9 blocks into the holes in the top side. Slide the other piece B onto the other side of the blocks. Nail into place. The blocks should now revolve on the dowel.
Paint the whole unit. Paint the sides of the blocks in contrasting colours. Cut and fix the felt into place.

3 Fix pins or numbers to the blocks.

The rules are on *page 39.*

Darts

You will need
4 cork floor tiles
  (about 40 cm square)
lengths of 45 × 25 mm wood
80 × 40 cm chipboard
hardboard
enamel and blackboard paint
paint brushes
drill
fretsaw
screws
screwdriver
number stencils
glue

1 Paint the board on one tile. Cut a square of hardboard 10 cm larger than the tile. Cut a hole the diameter of the board.

2 Screw the frame of the lengths of wood to the chipboard, leaving a gap at the bottom so the tiles can be pushed out of the pocket. Paint with blackboard paint. Fix on the hardboard front. Drill holes in the corners for hanging.

3 Paint the front with enamel. Stencil the numbers.

The rules for playing Darts are on *page 40.*

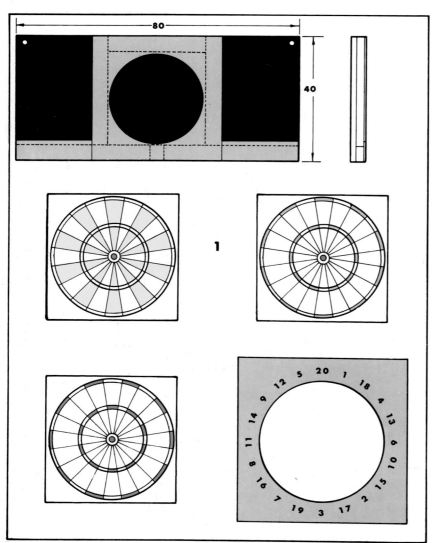

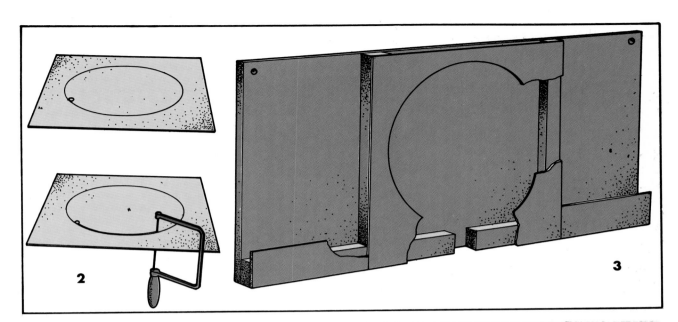

Skittles

You will need
plastic bottles
table tennis balls
enamel paint
paint brush
adhesive tape
a ball
sand or water (optional)

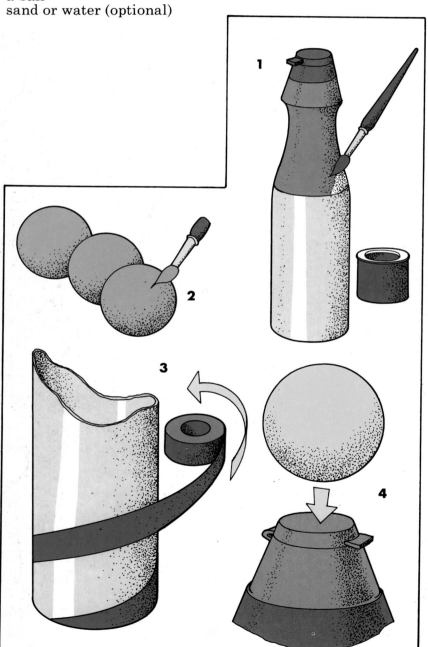

32

1 Paint the plastic bottles all over.

2 Paint a table tennis ball for each bottle in a contrasting colour.

3 Stick spirals of tape round the bottles as decoration.

4 Glue the table tennis balls to the top of the bottles.

If you want to make the skittles slightly heavier to knock down, experiment with filling them partly with sand or water.

You can use an ordinary rubber ball or tennis ball with your skittles. Set up the skittles in various different patterns and take it in turns to see how many you can knock down.

Jacob's Ladder

You will need
lengths of soft wood
fretsaw
sandpaper
1 cm wide cotton tape
glue

1 Cut 6 or more lengths of wood all exactly 10 cm long. Round the top and bottom ends slightly with the sandpaper.
Cut the tape into 16 cm lengths and fix them as alternate single centre and double side hinges joining the pieces as shown.

2 When all the wooden pieces are held together firmly, hold the top piece between your fingers and the second piece will seem to fall to the bottom of the ladder. Then invert the top piece and again the second piece will seem to fall. Pull the top piece back again and see what happens – for as long as you wish to try. See if you can work out what happens – for the game is an optical illusion.

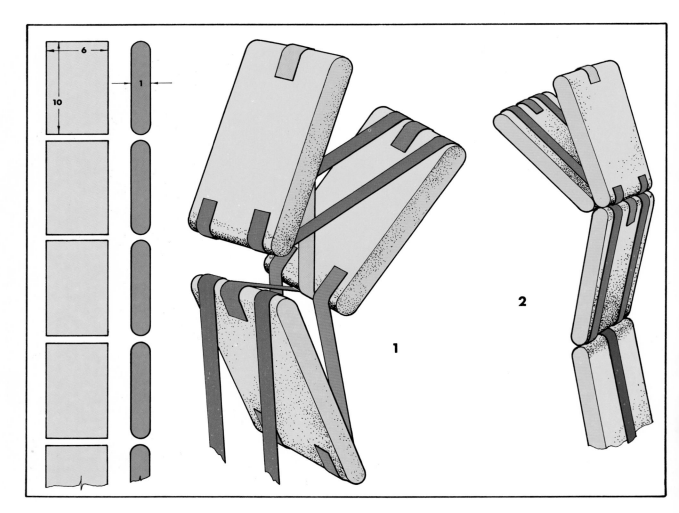

Rules

SOLITAIRE

1 This game for a solitary person was invented in France in the eighteenth century. The player puts 32 marbles or other markers on the board, leaving the centre hole empty.

2 The object of the game is to end with only one marble on the board – in the centre hole.

3 At each turn one marble must jump in a straight line over an adjacent marble to an empty space beyond. The marble which has been jumped over is taken off the board.

4 If you have tried to find the solution and given up, try this one.

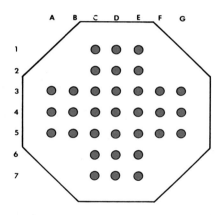

1.	D2 into D4 remove D3		
2.	F3	D3	E3
3.	E1	E3	E2
4.	E4	E2	E3
5.	C1	E1	D1
6.	E1	E3	E2
7.	E6	E4	E5
8.	G5	E5	F5
9.	D5	F5	E5
10.	G3	G5	G4
11.	G5	E5	F5
12.	B5	D5	C5
13.	C7	C5	C6
14.	C4	C6	C5
15.	E7	C7	D7
16.	C7	C5	C6
17.	C2	C4	C3
18.	A3	C3	B3
19.	D3	B3	C3
20.	A5	A3	A4
21.	A3	C3	B3
22.	D5	D3	D4
23.	D3	B3	C3
24.	B3	B5	B4
25.	B5	D5	C5
26.	D5	F5	E5
27.	F4	D4	E4
28.	C4	E4	D4
29.	E3	E5	E4
30.	F5	D5	E5
31.	D6	D4	D5

QUEEN'S GUARD

1 This is a game for 2 players. Each player has a Queen and 6 Guards of their own colour.

2 The pieces are placed on the board as shown here:

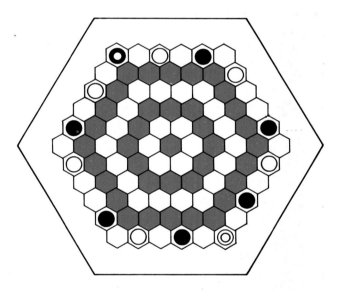

The object of the game is to place your Queen in the centre of the board with the 6 Guards around her.

3 The pieces move one hexagon at a time either towards the centre or sideways but never backwards.

4 No piece can move in between two enemy pieces. If a Guard becomes flanked by two enemy pieces in a line, at the next move it must be returned to the outer ring. If a Queen is so flanked, she must also be moved at the next turn, but she can go to any part of the board. If two or more pieces are flanked by the enemy, the Queen must be moved at the first turn and the other pieces in later turns.

5 Only a Queen can occupy the centre hexagon. If the Guards surround it, neither player can win.

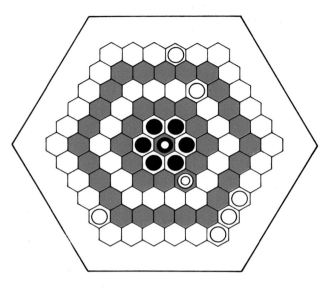

Some words of advice!
You won't win just by fighting off the enemy. Go full speed for centre. Try to throw back more than one enemy piece at a time. Don't let the Queen rush ahead too fast or she may get cut off.

DRAUGHTS

A variety of games can be played on a draughts board. Here are a few of them.

English Draughts or American Checkers

1 This is played on a board with 8 black and white squares up and across. Each player has 12 pieces which are all placed on and move on the black squares as shown.

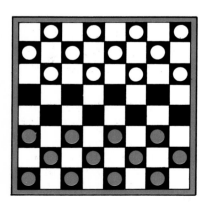

2 The objects of the game are to get one's men across the board and to capture or trap the opposing pieces.

3 Black always starts. The draughtsmen move diagon-

ally forward one square at a time. They may jump diagonally over one or a series of the opponent's men to a blank square beyond. The men jumped are taken off the board.

4 When a draughtsman reaches the opponent's back line or 'crownhead' it becomes a King, and is crowned with a spare draught. A King can move diagonally both backwards and forwards on the board. A King captures and is captured like an ordinary draughtsman.

5 If a player fails to take an enemy piece which is available, he pays one of these penalties:
a. The opponent may insist that the move be retaken correctly.
b. The move may be accepted, but the possible capture must be made on the next turn.
c. The opponent may remove the piece which should have made the capture. This is called 'Huffing'.

Continental Draughts

1 This game is played on a board of 10 x 10 squares with 20 black and 20 white pieces placed on the board as shown. It was described in the nineteenth century as 'a much more lively game than common draughts'.

2 Pieces can move one square diagonally forward, but they capture forwards and backwards diagonally.

3 Capturing is compulsory. If there is a choice of possible captures the player must take the line on which the greatest number or value of captures can be made. For instance, if the choice is between taking a draughtsman or a King, he must take the King.

4 A draughtsman is only crowned King when the move allows it to finish on the opposing back line. If more captures are possible backwards, the player must take them and wait to move to the 'crownhead' in another turn.

5 A King can move diagonally any number of vacant squares and can land any number of vacant squares beyond a piece it has captured.

6 Captured pieces are lifted at the end of a turn but cannot be jumped over more than once in that turn.

Reversi

1 Each player has 32 men, black on one side and red on the other. (You could put stickers on the reverse side of your draughts for this game.) One player uses black side uppermost, the other red. The game is played on an 8 x 8 square draughts board.

2 Black starts by placing a man on one of the four central squares. Then red places one, then black, then red, until the four squares are filled.

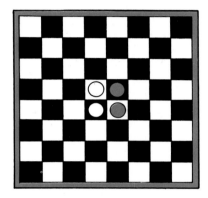

3 From then on each player must place his man on the board next to an enemy piece and in a straight line with one of his own men. If he cannot do so he loses his turn. A man which gets sandwiched on a straight line or diagonally between two opposing pieces is *reversed*, that is turned over so that it becomes the other player's colour and piece.

4 When all the squares on the board are covered, the player with the most pieces wins.

Turkish draughts

1 Correctly this game is played on a blank squared board of 8 x 8 squares. It can be played on an ordinary draughts board. The 16 draughtsmen on each side are positioned as shown.

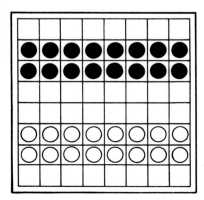

2 Pieces move one square in straight lines forward or sideways. Captures are made by jumping forward or sideways onto a vacant square. A series of jumps can be made in one move.

3 Pieces which reach the back line are crowned Kings. A King can move forward, backwards and sideways over any number of empty squares. After jumping a piece, a King can land on any vacant square in line behind that piece.

4 The player who captures or immobilizes all the opposing pieces or who reduces his opponent to one King and one draughtsman is the winner.

BACKGAMMON

The game uses a number of terms which can be simply mastered.
Points The board has two sides with two sets of 6 elongated triangles or *points* on each.
Bar The sets of points are separated by the *bar*.
Inner Table The player's first set of 6 points. *Outer Table* The second set of 6 points.

1 The game is played by 2 players each having 15 pieces and playing with 2 dice.

2 The object of the game is to bring all one's pieces into one's inner table, and assemble them there so that they can be *borne off* the board. The first player to do this is the winner.

3 The pieces are placed on the board as shown in the diagram. Traditionally the inner table is nearer the light.

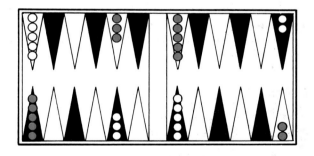

4 The players each throw one dice and the player with the highest score starts. He throws both dice for his moves.

5 The pieces are moved from the opponent's inner to outer table, then to the home outer table and finally to the home inner table. When they are all assembled there, they can be borne off the board.

6 The score on each dice may be used separately or totalled. But if the throw is totalled, the move on each dice must be possible. A player must play the whole throw if he can, but if not he loses all or part of it.

7 When a pair or *doublet* is thrown the player moves a combination of double the score. For example, a double 4 gives a move of 4+4+4+4.

8 When a player has 2 or more pieces (to a limit of 5) on one point he has *made a point* and the other player cannot move onto it.

9 If a single piece is on a point it is known as a *blot*. If an opponent's piece lands on that point, the blot is *hit* and is placed on the bar. It stays there until it can be played back into the opponent's inner table. A player can hit two or more blots in one throw.

10 If a piece is placed on the bar, the player cannot move any other piece until it has entered the game again. To do this the dice must be thrown to correspond to a point on the opponent's inner table not held by him. A player may lose several moves while he waits to re-enter a piece.

11 When all the pieces are assembled in the player's inner table, the player uses the throw of the dice as follows:
a To move pieces up the inner table.
b If a number higher than any point covered is thrown, a piece from the highest point may be borne off.
c If a number is thrown for an unoccupied point, no piece below it can be borne off if any piece remains above.
d With a doublet it may be possible to bear off 4 men with a single throw.

12 If a blot is hit while the player is bearing off his pieces, he must wait until that piece has re-entered and travelled round the board before any other pieces can be borne off.

MANCALA

This game, which has been popular for centuries in various forms across Africa and Asia, combines in its highest form a great deal of skill with numbers and at a lower level a very pleasant pastime for everyone from 5 upwards. It is ideal therapy for anyone who needs to exercise their hands and fingers (say, after an accident or because of rheumatism). We give here two forms of the game.

Game 1

1 The players sit facing each other across the board. The 6 wells on your side of the board belong to you and your opponent will try to capture the beads, seeds or acorns in these wells. Captured beads are stored in some boards in large wells on the board.

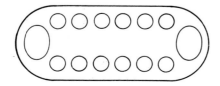

2 On your turn you pick up all 4 beads from one of your own wells and drop them one by one in a clockwise direction into each of the following wells round the board. If the last bead you play makes a total of 2 or 3 beads in one of your opponent's wells, you capture those beads. You also capture the beads in the previous wells on your opponent's side if one or more of them contain(s) only 2 or 3 beads too. When beads are captured they are taken off the board.

3 You must leave at least one piece on your opponent's side, but you may empty your own side. But when your own side is empty and you cannot play, your opponent takes all the pieces on his side. The winner is the person with the most beads at the end of the game.

Game 2

This game is easier to play if you do not use your numerical skill, but much more skilful if you can.

1 The players sit facing each other across the board. The 6 wells on your side of the board belong to you and your opponent will try to capture them.

2 On your turn you pick up all the beads from one of your own wells and drop them one by one in a clockwise direction into each of the following wells round the board as in game 1. If the final bead falls into an occupied well, you pick up *all* the beads which are now in that well and continue to drop them round the board. Your turn ends when you either make a new set of 4 with your final drop or your last bead drops in an empty well.

3 If your final drop of 4 is on your opponent's side you capture those 4 beads. At the end of every turn *both* players take off the board any new groups of 4 which have been left on their own side of the board. In some boards there is a well to store captured pieces.

4 The play continues in this way until the board is cleared or all the pieces are on one side, in which case they are taken by that player.

5 The player with the most groups of 4 wins. For the next game say one player has won 7 groups of 4, he now starts with his own 6 wells plus one on his opponent's side of the board. He may start to play from this well and may pick up groups of 4 in it. The ultimate aim is to capture all your opponent's wells.

WORD AND NUMBER FISH

1 This is a game for 2 or more players which teaches word or number recognition. You can prepare a pack of 12 or more pairs of cards (about 50 cards, 25 pairs, would be the maximum you would use at one time). Depending on how you have made your pack, a pair could be:

2 pictures, 2 words, 2 number spot 4's, 2 number and word 4's, 1 number spot 4 plus 1 number and word 4, 1 picture plus 1 word.

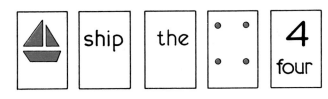

2 Deal seven cards to each player and put the remainder of the pack face down on the table. Players then find any pairs which they have been dealt in their hands and put them down.

3 Then the first player asks any other player, 'Have you got . . .? (naming a pair for a card in his hand). If the player asked has that card, he or she must hand it over. If he hasn't got it, he says 'Fish' and the other player 'fishes' a card from the pack and adds it to his hand. If it completes a pair, he may put that pair down. If the player asks for a card and gets it, he then lays down that pair and has another turn. When he has to 'fish', the turn goes onto the next player.

4 The player who gets all his cards down first is the winner.

This game is very useful to help 'fix' such words as in, out, the, and. It can also be used to teach word recognition in another language, either with pairs of words (*chat* and *chat*) or with the words in both languages (*chat* and *cat*).

SHOVE HA'PENNY

This old English game used to be played with half pennies or ha'pennies. Now a two pence piece is used.

1 The game is played by 2 players or 2 teams of 2 players each. Five coins are used.

2 For each player's turn the coins are placed one at a time over the near edge of the board and then 'shoved' with the palm of the hand or ball of the thumb up the board.

3 The aim of the game is to score 3 times in each 'bed', that is between each set of lines.

4 A coin which lies across a line is 'dead' unless it is knocked into a bed by a later coin.
A coin which passes beyond the beds is completely dead and should be taken out of play immediately so it cannot act as a 'buffer'. A coin which is knocked off a bed becomes dead unless it is moved into another bed. A coin which does not touch the first line can be replayed.

5 At the end of each turn, a peg is put in to score for each coin which lies in that bed. Once 3 coins have been scored for any one bed, that bed is filled and any more coins which end in that bed score for the other team (if they still need points in that bed). But a team must score its final winning point for itself.

6 No score is taken until all 5 coins have been played. If one coin lies on top of another, neither scores a point. The experienced player tries to fill the farthest beds first!

FLAP DICE

There are two games you can play on this board. For both you need 2 dice and you start with the numbers on the flaps facing upwards.

Game 1

The players take turns to throw the dice 6 times each, aiming to 'flap' over all the numbers by using the throw of the dice separately or combined. For example, if you throw 6 and 3, you can turn over *either* 6 and 3 *or* 9. On early throws it is better to go for the high numbers. The winner of each game is the person with the most numbers flapped over.

Game 2

The players throw the dice as in game 1, aiming to flap over all the numbers, but each player continues to throw until he is unable to use the throw of both dice. For example, the game might stand like this:

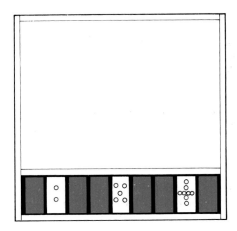

Your throw might be 6 and 4 so you could use neither dice, or 5 and 4 so you could only use one. Your turn is ended and the score against you is 258. The other player(s) aims to get a lower score. It is obviously best to cover high numbers as soon as possible.

DARTS

On a dart board each section scores as shown outside the circle. The outer circle on each section scores double and the inner circle, triple. The outer bull's eye scores 25 and the inner bull's eye scores 50.

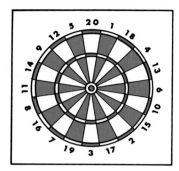

There are various games you can play on a dart board. The two most popular are probably 301 and Round the Clock.

301

1 This is a game for two players or two teams, each player throwing 3 darts on each turn.

2 The aim is to score exactly 301 ending on a double figure.

3 Each player or team must start by throwing a double in his first turn. All darts in that turn are then scored.

4 At the end of the game the players must end with a double. For instance, if you have 36 to get, you must aim for double 18. If you in fact score 20 in that turn, you then aim for double 8 in your next turn. If you have to get 3, you aim for 1 and a double 1.

Round the clock

1 The aim of this game is very simple: to score on all the numbers starting with 20 and ending with 1, with a final dart into the bull at the end. You can ignore the double and treble spaces for this game.